D1602649

Managing Conflict in the Family Business

A FAMILY
BUSINESS
PUBLICATION

Family Business Publications are the combined efforts of the Family Business Consulting Group and Palgrave Macmillan. These books provide useful information on a broad range of topics that concern the family business enterprise, including succession planning, communication, strategy and growth, family leadership, and more. The books are written by experts with combined experiences of over a century in the field of family enterprise and who have consulted with thousands of enterprising families the world over, giving the reader practical, effective, and time-tested insights to everyone involved in a family business.

FBCG, founded in 1994, is the leading business consultancy exclusively devoted to helping family enterprises prosper across generations.

FAMILY BUSINESS LEADERSHIP SERIES

This series of books is comprised of concise guides and thoughtful compendiums to the most pressing issues that anyone involved in a family firm may face. Each volume covers a different topic area and provides the answers to some of the most common and challenging questions.

Titles include:

Developing Family Business Policies: Your Guide to the Future
Effective Leadership in the Family Business
Family Business Compensation
Family Business Governance: Maximizing Family and Business Potential
Family Business Ownership: How to Be an Effective Shareholder
Family Business Succession: The Final Test of Greatness
Family Business Values: How to Assure a Legacy of Continuity and Success
The Family Constitution: Agreements to Secure and Perpetuate Your Family and Your Business
Family Education for Business-Owning Families: Strengthening Bonds by Learning Together
Family Meetings: How to Build a Stronger Family and a Stronger Business
Financing Transitions: Managing Capital and Liquidity in the Family Business
From Siblings to Cousins: Prospering in the Third Generation and Beyond
How Families Work Together
How to Choose and Use Advisors: Getting the Best Professional Family Business Advice
Working for a Family Business: A Non-Family Employee's Guide to Success
Letting Go: Preparing Yourself to Relinquish Control of the Family Business
Make Change Your Family Business Tradition
More than Family: Non-Family Executives in the Family Business
Nurturing the Talent to Nurture the Legacy: Career Development in the Family Business
Preparing Successors for Leadership: Another Kind of Hero
Preparing Your Family Business for Strategic Change
Siblings and the Family Business: Making It Work for Business, the Family, and the Future
Managing Conflict in the Family Business: Understanding Challenges at the Intersection of Family and Business

All of the books were written by members of the Family Business Consulting Group and are based on both our experiences with thousands of client families as well as our empirical research at leading research universities the world over.

Managing Conflict in the Family Business

Understanding Challenges at the Intersection of Family and Business

Kent Rhodes and David Lansky

palgrave
macmillan

MANAGING CONFLICT IN THE FAMILY BUSINESS

First published in 2013 by
PALGRAVE MACMILLAN®
in the United States—a division of St. Martin's Press LLC,
175 Fifth Avenue, New York, NY 10010.

Where this book is distributed in the UK, Europe and the rest of the world,
this is by Palgrave Macmillan, a division of Macmillan Publishers Limited,
registered in England, company number 785998, of Houndmills,
Basingstoke, Hampshire RG21 6XS.

Palgrave Macmillan is the global academic imprint of the above companies
and has companies and representatives throughout the world.

Palgrave® and Macmillan® are registered trademarks in the United States,
the United Kingdom, Europe and other countries.

ISBN: 978–1–137–27460–1

Library of Congress Cataloging-in-Publication Data

Rhodes, Kent.
    Managing conflict in the family business : understanding challenges at
the intersection of family and business / Kent Rhodes & David Lansky.
        p. cm.—(Family business leadership series)
    Includes bibliographical references.
    ISBN 978–1–137–27460–1 (alk. paper)
    1. Family-owned business enterprises—Management. 2. Interpersonal
conflict. 3. Businesspeople—Family relationships. 4. Work and family.
    I. Lansky, David. II. Title.

HD62.25.R48 2013
658.4′053—dc23   2012041142

A catalogue record of the book is available from the British Library.

Design by Newgen Imaging Systems (P) Ltd., Chennai, India.

First edition: April 2013

10 9 8 7 6 5 4 3 2 1

Printed in the United States of America.

Contents

LIST OF EXHIBITS vii

Introduction: A Primer to Managing Conflict in
Family Business. 1

1: Managing Conflict: The Balance of Family
and Business 7

2: Common Dilemmas That Can Lead to Conflict. 21

3: Guidelines for Dealing with Dilemmas That
Lead to Conflict 51

4: Create a Legacy for Future Generations 79

ADDITIONAL REFERENCES 101

ABOUT THE AUTHORS. 103

INDEX 105

Exhibits

Exhibit 1.1
Four Reasons Why Working Together in a Family
Business Is Challenging 10

Exhibit 2.1
Reducing the Dilemmas Concerning Compensation
and Ownership. 26

Exhibit 2.2
Guidelines for How to "Avoid" Avoiding Conflict 30

Exhibit 2.3
Five Unwanted Effects of Triangulating 34

Exhibit 2.4
Guidelines for Managing Triangulation 36

Exhibit 2.5
How to Minimize Bullying and Scapegoating 39

Exhibit 2.6
How to Minimize the Negative Effects of Sibling Rivalry . . . 45

Exhibit 3.1
Assessing Your Conflict Management Skills:
Ten Reflection Questions 57

Exhibit 3.2
Steps for Listening Well 60

Exhibit 3.3
Key Elements to Ensuring a Fair Process 64

Exhibit 3.4
Establishing Policies and Structures That Benefit
Business and Family 67

Exhibit 3.5
Eight Steps to Better Communication 75

Exhibit 3.6
Ground Rules for Family Meetings 76

Exhibit 4.1
Align Vision and Mission to Manage Future Tensions. . . .84

Exhibit 4.2
Suggestions for Dealing with Destructive Entitlement . . .86

Exhibit 4.3
Seven Steps to Aid in Managing Conflicts More
Effectively in Family Businesses 89

Exhibit 4.4
Steps That Lead to Reconciliation 96

Introduction: A Primer to Managing Conflict in Family Business

This book identifies patterns of family business tensions, dilemmas, and conflicts and offers practical guidelines for managing them more effectively. It is written as a primer to better understand the unique juncture of family and business, describing the most common tensions and dilemmas that business-owning families tend to encounter and then providing options for helping families stay ahead of them.

Business-owning families and the professionals who study them and work with them recognize that conflicts are a part of the ongoing cycle of business management and ownership. The intersection of family dynamics with business dynamics provides for potentially volatile and destructive conflicts. The good news for business-owning families is that conflicts don't have to be volatile *or* destructive. Identifying, understanding, and preparing to manage these unique tensions and dilemmas can help ensure future success for the family and business. Even more important, understanding the predictable occurrence and proper management of certain dilemmas can help a family grow its business, enhance relationships, and secure a higher commitment to the family legacy.

Therefore, the goal of this book is to help families manage conflict so that family *and* business can survive, grow, succeed, and thrive. At a fundamental level, this book presents core principles, scenarios, and tactics for understanding and addressing the common tensions and dilemmas that occur when families simultaneously work to build multigenerational businesses, join together to give back to their communities in shared philanthropy, and collectively build shared financial assets that benefit both the family as a whole and its members.

But this primer is also a practical guide, providing information to help equip families owning businesses to *manage* some of those more common conflicts in ways that uphold both family relationships and the business. Its purpose is to help families think about how to tolerate, accept, and successfully live with the occasional less-than-ideal situation rather than letting tension between family members become a chronic ongoing dilemma, hoping it will just go away. Of course, many conflicts can and should actually be resolved, and the process and skill involved in effectively managing chronic conflicts are important first steps to resolution over time. To that end, this book seeks to provide business-owning families with tools to recognize common tensions, dilemmas, and conflicts and to help them identify where the problems come from; potentially, families can thus head off problems at the pass before they become full-blown conflicts. By applying these unique management skills, balancing both business and family can become a clearer process that also moves families to work at resolving conflicts.

It is important to note that learning and applying the tools for effective conflict management is a task for the *entire* family, not just any one person or even one generation. If you really want to resolve conflict, it's important to work toward what's good for the family as a whole and for all of the stakeholders, rather than ensuring that any one person achieves what he or she wants. Focusing on both family relationships and business goals is an important step.

The three core goals for families wishing to manage tensions and conflicts more effectively are:

1. understanding some of the coping tactics family members may use to deal with conflicts—tactics that are typically unsuccessful and may make the conflict worse,
2. recognizing some of the most common conflicts in business families (because your tensions and challenges are not unique), and
3. understanding better how to approach and work through chronic conflicts so they don't destroy either family relationships or the business.

Of course, there's no one-size-fits-all solution for families. Although most families face similar challenges, every family needs to find its own unique way of dealing with those challenges, because every family is different, and many families deal with the same type of conflict in radically different ways. By developing a process that best benefits *your* family and *your* business, you can begin to minimize and manage the conflicts that could otherwise get in the way of your business and your relationships.

To start with, this book also takes a realistic approach to the unique challenges that families face when they strive to work together, to share assets, and to perpetuate a legacy for the generations to follow. We focus on

- identifying and understanding sources of conflict so that they can be managed before outright conflicts occur,
- developing language regarding the types of conflicts unique to family enterprises,
- offering options for addressing these conflicts,
- realistically appraising and addressing conflicts that in all likelihood cannot be resolved in a reasonable period of time, and
- teasing out the opportunities for learning and growth that addressing conflicts can offer business-owning families.

Drawing on the disciplines of family psychology, management science, and corporate governance, this book explains how business-owning and other asset-sharing families can create and sustain success by effectively managing and leveraging conflicts that are predictable though not inevitable. As such, this hands-on guide has been compiled to benefit families who own businesses and share other assets, nonfamily managers, business school students and professors, management consultants, and other service providers (such as law firms, wealth-management firms, CPAs, and others) who routinely serve family-owned businesses.

Chapter 1

Managing Conflict: The Balance of Family and Business

The family unit is—and always has been throughout the world—the core operational group of society. It is also the primary vehicle for carrying on a business as a way to support that family unit. Today, in addition to owning and managing shared businesses, many successful families also collaborate in managing family offices, overseeing philanthropic endeavors through established family foundations or sharing control of other public and private enterprises. While all of these forms of family collaboration face similar challenges, the unique qualities of a family at the center of these structures add complexity to effectively balancing these challenges with the tensions and problems that come with being a family in business together.

Many conflicts in family businesses or enterprising families are *predictable*, but they are not necessarily *inevitable*. By focusing on helping family members and other interested parties associated with a family-owned enterprise to recognize those predictable conflicts, you can more accurately determine which of those conflicts might be headed off, brought to resolution, or managed over the long haul. The relevant management strategies can be implemented with the goal of simultaneously upholding the family and the business.

Exhibit 1.1 sums up the reasons why working together in a family business is challenging.

The bottom line is that some of the most challenging conflicts in family businesses often are not only complex but the result of long-term processes and developments rather than one-time events. For example, two brothers haven't spoken for years because of an old disagreement, an adult child has cut herself off from family gatherings because of a previous quarrel,

---

EXHIBIT 1.1   Four Reasons Why Working Together in a Family Business Is Challenging

1. Being engaged with each other in a family enterprise adds an entirely different level of complexity.
2. Family members may be uncomfortable with conflict and develop habits of coping with tensions that keep conflicts from surfacing.
3. Family members exhibit a reflex reaction to a problem that can blow the problem out of proportion.
4. The dilemmas arising when families live and work together add a layer of potential tensions that must be managed on a daily basis.

divorce brings pain to family relationships, etc. But unaddressed conflicts in a family can eventually erode relationships between family members to the point where conflict-ridden interactions with each other become accepted and family members consider them "normal." Although this otherwise relatively harmless dynamic can be found in most families, the added stress and responsibilities of interacting in the context of a business can make the conflict worse over time so that it can potentially become quite destructive.

In addition, many siblings and cousins working together in family businesses likely experience an *intimacy paradox*. This means that those siblings or cousins know each other so well that they are also skilled at knowing how to best interact with each other in ways that *avoid* conflict; unfortunately, this skill gets in the way when they need to have deeper conversations that might be uncomfortable to them. They know how to enjoy each other's company, but they also tacitly know what they shouldn't discuss or allude to because of its potential to create conflict. Many people develop these communication patterns and unspoken "don't go there" agreements when they are very young. The intimacy paradox arises when those old patterns of relating to each other begin to prevent family members who are working together in a family business from recognizing and discussing conflicts that affect the business and family relationships.

When business conflict is properly addressed, owners or managers tackle smaller challenges, managing them effectively in real time. But when events are not well managed or are accepted as normal or just ignored, they can become chronic, accumulate over time, and develop into crisis points. In family businesses with long or multigenerational histories and strong emotional ties, recognizing and managing conflict may be more challenging for family members than for non-family employees.

Yet, managing conflict is a challenge in any business setting and when approached correctly, some conflicts can actually be beneficial because they can push business leaders to see a situation differently or come to a deeper understanding of people and circumstances that inform their decisions. Knowing how to manage conflict and then leverage it into an advantage is not always easy, however, and this is particularly true in families—and perhaps particularly in families who are also in business together or engage in other collaborative enterprises, such as a family office or a family foundation. That's because the dynamics that can produce conflict in a family combine with the challenges of owning and operating a business, introducing emotional and historical dynamics that may complicate solutions and opportunities. These conflicts can be more accurately described as dilemmas—situations in which tensions chronically exist and few clear answers are readily available without unwanted consequences for the family or the business. Learning to recognize and live with apparent dilemmas, polarities, and paradoxes is the key to successfully managing conflicts in the family enterprise.

According to experts, conflict is "a process that begins when an individual or group perceives differences and opposition between itself and another individual or group about interests and resources, beliefs, values, or practices that matter to them."[1] Although that definition is accurate, it is insufficient to describe the dilemmas and tensions that are common to families jointly involved in businesses and enterprises. In these contexts, every instance of conflict is further complicated by the multiple roles and relationships of family members. The CEO of a family enterprise may be the son of its founder, and he may also be dad to several children and granddad to several grandchildren. He is likely the husband of a spouse who helped him build the business and raise those children. He may be a brother to a vice president in the company or even a copresident with a sibling. In addition to being uncle to his siblings' children, he may also be their boss if they work in the family enterprise. Other dynamics may also be at work:

+ multiple family members may be working in the enterprise to make it successful and to provide for their individual families
+ other family members not active in the business may be owners or shareholders
+ the "permanency" of the relationships between family members
+ the role of in-laws and the relationships created across the family

---

[1] C. K. W. De Dreu, F. Harinck, and A. E. M. Van Vianen, "Conflict and Performance in Groups and Organizations," in Cooper and Robertson (eds.), *International Review of Industrial and Organizational Psychology* 14 (1999): 369–414.

Clearly, families working together in a business or enterprise also have to juggle the relationship between that enterprise and the family as a whole. This is true of family businesses on a global scale and across cultures, whether family members are engaged in the enterprise as owners or managers or both.

Every family business faces some conflict at one time or another and regarding many different situations. Whenever people work together, there are bound to be different opinions and ideas on how to get things done. Different opinions don't necessarily lead to conflict, but when different opinions combine with emotion, intransigence, criticism, or contempt, that's when conflict per se emerges.

Nevertheless, just because a family faces conflict doesn't mean it can't function well, because all conflicts can be managed, even though they may not be quickly or easily *resolved*. That's an important distinction, because business families don't actually approach conflicts in the same ways other organizations do. If you're working in a family business, it's likely you already recognize that your conflicts are something of a balancing act and that learning to work through conflicts may be more important than just trying to resolve them or get rid of them.

In addition, many families may not realize there's a significant problem in the business until it affects family relationships. Some families say they were motivated to seek help in managing conflicts because they recognized they were becoming less inclined to spend time with each other as a family away from the office. Some families in business may actually be closer than families that don't work together: families in business often vacation together, go on cruises or to the beach, the mountains, or a lake property; they go skiing, scuba diving, fishing, or just relax together as a large, extended family. When those vacations or long weekends are no longer fun for some or all family members, and they find themselves thinking "I just don't want to be around him [or her] any more than I have to," that's when the family realizes its relationships are starting to fray. And most families in business together don't want that to happen to their family *or* to their business.

THE THREE DOMAINS OF FAMILY BUSINESS

Figure 1.1 illustrates three general domains of family-owned businesses and the interaction between these domains. Each domain represents a "hat" a family member or other stakeholder might be wearing at any given time and the potential dilemmas or paradoxes that could be encountered in each role. One person might be dad and also CEO and a majority shareholder at different times; his son or daughter might be COO and a minority shareholder. These different constituencies and their interacting relationships result in interest groups, which might naturally be in conflict or competition because of differing agendas and priorities.

For example, how can you be boss and brother (or sister) at the same time? How can a brother and sister, with all the typical experiences of growing up together, put aside those sibling

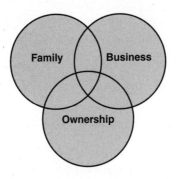

Figure 1.1   The Three Domains of Family Business.

Source: R. Tagiuri and J.A. Davis (1982) reprinted in Family Business Review, Vol. 9, No. 2 Summer, 1996 199–208. Sage Publications.

relationships and now focus on their business relationships, which may be those of CEO and COO? Or how do you balance the wish of family owners to have greater dividends when family business managers want to reinvest in the company? These overlapping roles and relationships create natural dilemmas that are accepted as part of a business-owning family's day-to-day life. But they also present opportunities for tensions and conflicts to emerge.

Successful business families manage to balance the needs of these interest groups and to keep the domains separate through clear boundaries:

1. They operate their businesses according to best business practices, while minimizing the influence of potentially competing family interests.

2. They strive to maintain harmony in their families while managing to keep business differences from affecting relationships.

3. They successfully create time and space at home that isn't about the business.

4. They act as responsible shareholders and stakeholders in the best interest of the enterprise.

To manage these domains successfully, you need to keep in mind which hat you are wearing as you make various decisions about your business or your family, and you need to make sure that decisions are made with the right interests in mind. Moreover, because many difficulties and conflicts are caused by lack of clarity, it helps to clarify at any given moment which hat you're wearing when you're interacting with your family in a business situation.

In general, the first-generation founders of a business (G1) have less need to keep the domains separate because a single founder tends to occupy all roles; therefore, there is (obviously) relatively little complexity in this regard. However, as a family expands to the second generation (G2) and third generation (G3), the complexity increases exponentially, and the potential for conflicts increases similarly.

Thoughtful dialogue about differing—or competing—agendas coupled with clear policies can help families to balance these interest groups and their responsibilities in each domain. The discussion in this book on conflict management techniques and guidelines can be helpful to families who must deal with these naturally competing interest groups in the three domains of family business.

It's important to keep in mind that each of the domains in these three circles will change over time. The business will change: it will grow, and it may contract. For example, you may acquire other businesses, or you may spin off or close out segments of your business. Similarly, your family will change in the natural cycle of life, with marriages, births, perhaps divorces, and, eventually, deaths. Even the business ownership will change over time. All three circles are dynamic, and this adds to the complexity of the relationships among the three domains. If you recognize these changes, though, you'll be better equipped to handle the challenges—and possible conflicts—that may arise from those changes.

ELIMINATING CONFLICTS OR MANAGING CONFLICTS: WHAT'S REALISTIC?

Many families want conflict to just go away. There's even support for this idea in some of the popular literature on conflict resolution, along the lines of "all you have to do is compromise, and everything will be fine." But there's not a lot of information on how to get a group of people who are related to each other and also work together in a significant enterprise to understand that *compromise is not the same as collaboration.* In a compromise each individual gives up something of value in order to keep the peace, but collaboration goes beyond that and means accepting and tolerating differences while committing to work together to find a yet-to-be-created solution. This takes dedication and hard work, but it is generally seen as a rewarding process for everyone involved.

For example, in one business family, dad (the business founder) disagreed with his son's decision to acquire a new business, and their discussions had deteriorated into long sessions of anger and rhetoric. In striving to resolve their conflict, they agreed that as CEO, the son had the authority to decide on new business acquisitions. So, while dad did not agree with the decision and did not participate in the acquisition, he allowed it to go forward without further interference. Dad did not compromise—he did not even agree—but he recognized that he would need to accept his son's authority, and he did so. In the end, both parties truly benefitted, because son saw that he could exert authority effectively in spite of dad's opposition, and dad realized that he didn't have to be involved in every new business activity.

> There's rarely an "aha" experience in working through conflicts.
> Instead, effectively managing conflicts includes a *process* of recognizing the common dilemmas inherent in being associated with a family business and working to address long-entrenched patterns of behavior that may have developed as a result.

There's rarely a moment in working through conflicts where a single answer is suddenly clear. Rather, putting a process in place that enables you and your family to recognize patterns and behaviors that may cause conflict and learning how to address those issues will help head off potentially harmful results. Family relationships are the most long-term relationships you're ever going to have; for example, sibling relationships typically last longer than relationships with parents or even spouses. Your way of interacting with your family has literally been a lifelong process that you're not going to change from one moment to the next. However, family members can learn new behaviors by first noticing their own *patterns* of behavior in the context of the dilemmas they are facing in the family enterprise.

Learning to manage conflict effectively is important for anyone involved with a business family—whether you're the founder and want to turn your business over to your children, or a member of the second generation working with (and trying to get along with) parents, siblings, and brothers and sisters-in-law, or a member of the third or later generation trying to maintain the legacy of previous generations while looking to the future and working within a large and ever-growing network of family relationships.

Chapter 2

Common Dilemmas That Can Lead to Conflict

COMPENSATION AND OWNERSHIP

Because individuals in a business family simultaneously balance their roles as family members, owners, and managers, decisions made from the point of view of one role may conflict with decisions made from another one. This is particularly apparent when families in business try to resolve tensions by being both fair *and* equal, which all parents know is an important rule in rearing children. Indeed, parents will most assuredly hear about it when that rule is not upheld. But those two words—fair and equal—don't mean the same thing, particularly in dealing with adults and work situations. In fact, those two goals are sometimes even mutually exclusive.

Separate the issue of compensation for working *in* the business from the rewards of ownership distributed *from* the business.

Thus, it may not be appropriate for all family members who are working in the business to receive the same compensation simply because they are family members or even owners; instead, they should be compensated according to the level of jobs they have and their level of qualification for their jobs. To structure compensation equally for next-generation employees without regard to job qualification and fit typically feeds rivalry and jealousy in subsequent generations. (For more information regarding compensation see *Family Business Compensation* by Craig Aronoff, Stephen McClure, and John Ward.)

For example, three second-generation siblings working in the business have different management roles and responsibilities. The eldest daughter is running the family enterprise as CEO, and one of her younger brothers is in charge of sales while the other oversees production. They may be equal owners in terms of share distribution, but their compensation—and how it is structured—is quite different. While this approach is certainly fair, it is not necessarily equal: The daughter who is running the company will likely be making a competitive salary with a potential bonus structure based on company success, whereas her brother who is overseeing sales will be compensated with an annual draw and with a commission structure that rewards him when sales targets are met or exceeded. The third sibling overseeing production is most likely to earn compensation that is in line with industry standards for that type of position.

When positions and responsibilities in a company are different, the people working in those positions will likely be compensated differently, depending on job scope and responsibility—and that makes sense to you when you are wearing your "business hat." But when the parents are wearing their "family hats," they may view their three children's compensation as unfair because it is different based on each individual's role *as employee* rather than on siblings' roles as owners. In fact, those siblings may have the same sort of view: "Gee, Dad, you love my sister so much more than you love me!" or "I own the same percentage of this company as they do!" Thus, this common scenario not only results in potential tension between parent and child but also among the three siblings.

A good way to decrease the tensions caused by the fair and equal dilemma is to create a compensation policy for family members working in the firm, with an understanding that compensation for family members working in the business should be carefully planned and spelled out. These guidelines might include compensation approaches that are in line with other companies' pay practices that are in the same industry, geographic location, and size category. Decisions need to be made as to how family members will be paid in relation to the market value for the industry, job function, education levels, and work or management experience. In other words, a clear plan should be developed to prepare each family member to work in the family business based on market-driven factors and to ensure that each family member has the necessary experience and education for a particular job in the family business, just as he or she would need for a job in any other company in that industry.

Thus, an adult child wanting to work in the family business shouldn't become the CFO even if she's a wiz at arithmetic if she has no formal finance training or experience. Likewise, her brother shouldn't be the HR director despite having good people skills if he has not finished college and just needs a job. All management positions in a business require professional development, experience, and education; providing clear pathways for family members interested in career placement with the family enterprise will decrease the likelihood of future tensions in the family and the business. Keep in mind that what is best for the business is usually best for the family, and create a clear plan for family members that identifies appropriate available positions in the company, while also providing a more comfortable and effective job match. Exhibit 2.1 offers a few guidelines for reducing dilemmas concerning compensation and ownership of the business.

EXHIBIT 2.1   Reducing the Dilemmas Concerning Compensation and Ownership

- Determine compensation based on industry standards for specific positions.
- Separate the idea of owner benefits (distributions, share value, etc.) from compensation derived from employment in the business.
- Create compensation plans for family members working in the business that are in line with other management positions in the business.
- Separate compensation for working in the business from rewards associated with ownership.
- Make estate plans clear early on.

AVOIDING CONFLICT

Many of the dilemmas faced by families in business are rooted in the fact that most families are naturally averse to conflict. In fact, most people prefer stability and harmony in their relationships. But that's not always possible in life in general, in families, or in businesses. But it is also important to understand that it is often during times of most difficulty that people and families can grow in their capacity to solve problems and overcome challenges. Therefore, acknowledging difficulties and striving to manage conflict in a family can be an important growth experience for individuals and their families.

However, many families refrain from acknowledging the presence of conflict in their relationships because they believe that acknowledging the difficulty might "open Pandora's box" and make things worse than they already are. Therefore, these families become very skilled at *conflict avoidance*. While conflict avoidance makes some things better in the short term (i.e., by making relationships seem relatively harmonious), it will create deeper dilemmas in the long term.

For business families, however, conflict and conflict avoidance are more urgent and potentially more toxic phenomena: the family's livelihood, employee stakeholders, communities, and family legacy are all threatened by conflict and by ineffectual efforts to avoid it. Thus, business families have a higher stake in identifying conflict when it occurs, preventing it if possible, and knowing when avoiding a conflict is actually making it worse. However, even when conflict is acknowledged and recognized and when there is a commitment to address it head-on rather than ignore it, dealing with that conflict may be challenging because often the fundamental issues or underlying troubles are difficult to observe or understand. Often, families find themselves dealing with the *symptoms* of a problem rather than the core of the conflict itself.

> Part of managing conflict well lies in the commitment to accept change, to understand that it will have an impact, and to explore how change in family or business affects key stakeholders.

In one family business, there was constant tension between the father and his two sons, all of whom worked in the business. No business matter could be addressed without the older son expressing his dissatisfaction with the outcome. This continued for a long time until the younger son finally persuaded his brother and father to meet in order to discuss the friction. During the course of their meeting, the older son expressed his disappointment that his younger brother had been named dad's successor as president of the company. Until their meeting, the family had never discussed the father's decision. Dad had simply announced it a year earlier. In an effort to keep the peace, the older son kept silent about having been passed over in the succession plan. However, keeping silent did not eliminate his unhappiness—it merely came to be expressed in other ways in day-to-day management.

When people keep silent about an important dissatisfaction in their lives, the issue may continue to fester internally. As psychologist Carl Jung said:

> *"Everyone carries a shadow, and the less it is embodied in the individual's conscious life, the blacker and denser it is. If [a problem] is conscious, one always has a chance to correct it.... But if it is repressed and isolated from consciousness, it never gets corrected and is liable to burst forth suddenly in a moment of unawareness.... At all counts, it forms an unconscious snag, thwarting our most well-meant intentions."*[1]

The act of avoidance or suppression can itself become a central organizing factor or theme of a relationship. Staying silent—keeping something in your "shadow"—helps to avoid one sort of conflict, but then the conflict can be expressed in other ways that actually are more damaging to family and business relationships than talking about the original hurt or misunderstanding. *Thus, it is often what people don't say that may have the most impact on their relationships and create the biggest dilemmas.*

Not every difficult event or hurt from the past can or should be discussed in the present; often, silence *is* golden. So how do you know whether the silence should be broken, whether the "shadow" material should be expressed? And is there a preferred

---

[1] Carl Jung, "Psychology and Religion," in *Psychology and Religion: West and East*, vol. 11 of *Collected Works* (London: Routledge and Kegan Paul, 1938, repr. 1958), 131.

method for doing so? Although there is no one answer that fits every situation, family members can become a little more sensitized to the occurrence of continual underlying tension in a relationship, because when tension is clearly and consistently evident and no one talks about it, that is when silence may *not* be golden. The need to address unspoken issues should also be recognized when reasonable people seem unable to arrive at reasonable agreements. Exhibit 2.2 offers additional guidelines.

EXHIBIT 2.2   Guidelines for How to "Avoid" Avoiding Conflict

1. Commit to creating a culture or "norm" that genuinely invites appropriate one-on-one discussions when tension begins to build in family relationships.
2. Consider bringing in an outside, third-party facilitator when necessary and appropriate.
3. Avoid substituting talking to others instead of talking with the person with whom you experience tension.
4. Work to identify why it is important to discuss difficult matters. Is it to clarify the reasons for a decision or to arrive at a more durable solution to a problem? Therefore, do some planning before the discussion and make sure all parties are aware of the goals before you start.
5. Set a specific time and place for the discussions.

6. Set a time limit; if you find during a meeting that you need more time to discuss this issue, schedule another time to continue the discussion.

7. Strive to create a communication atmosphere that is safe for all parties—where open and genuine sharing result in compassionate listening, not defensive criticism.

8. Remember that the most important parts of the process are listening and generating solutions. Avoid attributing blame or responsibility for the conflict or problem.

9. Keep the process private. Agree that the content of these meetings remains confidential.

Staying silent is, of course, not the only way that families avoid conflict. Some people try to cope with potentially difficult situations by physically leaving or physically avoiding potential problem situations, or by working around potentially difficult situations or family members.

For example, in one family succession planning had become a very heated issue between two cousins. Other family members, none of whom were active in the business, left it to their two feuding cousins to resolve the issue. Although one (female) cousin was clearly the best-suited candidate for the job, another (male) cousin thought they should create a copresident leadership structure. This male cousin had become so forceful in his arguments, and communication between the two cousins had become so problematic, that his female cousin simply avoided him—she left meetings when he raised his voice, she stopped taking his phone calls, she took circuitous routes around the plant to ensure she did not come anywhere near his office, and so on.

Although her actions did help to reduce the tension she felt in her interactions with her male cousin, she certainly didn't solve the problem of succession or poor communication. Moreover, her physical avoidance of the situation only resulted in her male cousin's being angry about her physically avoiding him and intensifying his efforts to convince her that he was right when he did have the occasional opportunity to address the matter. So the conflict has been avoided but not eliminated, and it certainly hasn't been resolved.

Another way families tend to avoid conflict is by simply working around it. They find other ways to get things done, without involving the people with whom conflict usually occurs. For example, the family might have meetings and make decisions without a difficult person present. In some cases, a difficult family member may *seem* to be involved, but his or her opinions are not taken seriously. In other cases, a work-around might involve having another party take on the work that the difficult family member is not doing. Once again, however, work-arounds might bring an immediate sense of peace but the core problem remains unresolved.

> When tension is clearly and consistently evident, and no one talks about it, silence is *not* golden.

When family members understand that they are simply avoiding rather than addressing and resolving conflict, they can focus their efforts on creating a process to constructively manage the situation. Bringing in an objective third party or asking, "What might be going on here?" can help move the family from avoiding conflict to addressing its underlying causes. Asking questions about the *result* and *outcome* of avoiding conflict or working around it can highlight the dilemmas created over time. For example, rather than talking through difficult differences, two brothers stop socializing as much with their families, and their relationship is impaired; two cousins have been working around a third family member by holding "unofficial" meetings without him in order to minimize confrontation. The unwanted result is an increased level of mistrust among the three family members and diminished respect from employees.

It is not unusual for change itself to be an underlying source of conflict in a family because change upsets the status quo and requires a realignment of relationships, responsibilities, and expectations. By asking what has changed recently and how the family has been affected by that change families can further explore the factors underlying the dilemmas they are striving to manage.

An important part of managing conflict well lies in the commitment to accept change, to understand that it will have an impact, and to explore how change in either family or business affects key stakeholders.

TRIANGULATION

Triangulation is a common practice in families that creates dilemmas both in the present and for the future. Triangulation refers to a situation in which conflict between family members is managed independently by any or all of them by talking to a third party.

This third party then becomes a sounding board, relieving some of the tension and dissipating negative emotion in the short term. But when conflict in a family becomes chronic or recurrent and when triangulation is a frequent coping tactic, it will simply make some problems worse, creating dilemmas for everyone involved.

For example, when a triangulated person attempts to resolve a difficult situation by interceding on behalf of the family member who has been talking with him or her about a conflict, the triangulated person may then actually become a part of the conflict that he or she tries to resolve and even make it worse, as explained in exhibit 2.3.

EXHIBIT 2.3   Five Unwanted Effects of Triangulating

Triangulated family members have several challenges when stepping in to "help" in a conflict that can make matters worse and can create new dilemmas for the family:

1. They could make decisions that are one-sided due to a biased selection of facts.
2. They may be perceived as "sticking their nose where it doesn't belong."
3. They will be viewed as biased and "playing favorites."
4. They could take too much of the stress of the conflict upon themselves.
5. They may unintentionally be "siphoning" off the impetus for the parties to talk directly to each other to manage or resolve the conflict.

In one family, for example, the father no longer worked in the business but was often triangulated by each of his sons, one of whom was CEO and the other head of sales. They were frequently in conflict because the older son resisted his CEO younger brother's demands to comply with new "more professional" company guidelines in conducting performance evaluations for the employees reporting to him. In his mind, the move to formal evaluations limited his ability to manage his sales force based on the relationships he had built with each of them.

After being consulted many times by his older son who complained relentlessly about the CEO's "bullying" tactics, the father, who was now a triangulated party, interceded by demanding that his younger son stop his "bullying" and stop requiring the older son to conduct the performance evaluations. Not unexpectedly, conflict erupted between dad and the CEO, who asked dad to mind his own business since he no longer worked in the company and did not understand the impact that his brother's oppositional behavior was having on nonfamily employees.

> The best thing a triangulated party can do is to encourage those who are in conflict to speak directly to each other.

Being able to label triangulation when it occurs is a significant first step in managing it properly. Ultimately, the parties in conflict need to communicate directly and productively with each other. As long as the two parties in conflict are not actually talking to each other, resolving the original problem may not be possible. Family members (or others) who find that they are frequently triangulated need to resist the temptation to "help" in these difficult situations. Exhibit 2.4 offers additional guidelines on how to manage the dilemma of triangulation.

EXHIBIT 2.4   Guidelines for Managing Triangulation

- Getting advice from a trusted manager or family member may be a good practice, but resolving to talk directly to the other person will limit the dilemmas produced by triangulation alone.

- Separate the need to have a trusted person serve as a sounding board to help craft difficult conversations with others or to think through an appropriate response from a knee-jerk complaint to a family member that may relieve initial tension but also removes the incentive or energy to resolve the problem.

- The person acting as a sounding board likely hears only one point of view and may unknowingly support and solidify that one person's view even though there are always at least two sides to every story. Therefore, it is important to be committed to "fight your own battles" rather than hoping the person being triangulated will also take up your complaint and straighten out the person you are in conflict with.

♦ The person acting as a sounding board may well experience stress and discomfort because of the position that he or she is being put in. This is particularly true if the person being triangulated is a parent or sibling. If talking to a third party is necessary, it is best to get help outside of the business and the family from a trusted advisor or counselor.

BULLYING AND SCAPEGOATING

Bullying and scapegoating are defense tactics used to avoid taking personal responsibility for events, decisions, and conflicts, but they also create tensions and conflicts by themselves. Because of its lasting negative impacts on individuals and groups, bullying has received a great deal of attention in the media in recent years. And while it may not be typically thought of in connection with family businesses, it does show up in those contexts in much more *subtle* ways than the stereotypical schoolyard bully stealing lunch money. Bullying in family business occurs when a family member works to suppress or redirect conflict by *dictating* to other members of the family or working to exert control over them. When this occurs, the family business bully typically doesn't want another person to raise difficult issues, and he or she prevents that from happening through intimidation. In some cases, bullying can even seem relatively harmless, as when humor is constantly used to achieve the desired outcomes.

This type of subtle bullying in family businesses sometimes occurs in situations where gender is also an issue, for example, when male siblings may intimidate their sister(s) by routinely ignoring her or their suggestions or comments. But it's not uncommon for the same dynamic to exist across family relationships with the same result, affecting family relationships over time and creating new dilemmas that limit leadership choices for the family enterprise, impede the professional development of family members, and hinder effective ownership behaviors in the future.

Scapegoating is another way many families ineffectively attempt to deal with conflict. It deflects conflict by blaming another person for something negative that has happened or something that has gone wrong. Sometimes that person is responsible; sometimes he or she may have contributed to the problem or mistake, and sometimes that person wasn't involved at all, and the scapegoating is a complete fiction. The essence of scapegoating is blame, and what it does is allow a family member to blame someone else for his or her own problems.

> Scapegoating simultaneously sidesteps the true origins of a conflict and keeps family members from identifying the real cause of a problem. Over time, this approach actually increases conflict.

Scapegoating is distinct from holding others accountable for specific behaviors or decisions, which is an appropriate role for a manager. When scapegoating occurs in families, it may even be due to a long-standing role assigned to the family member who routinely seems to be blamed. Scapegoating simultaneously side-steps the true origins of a conflict and keeps family members from identifying the real cause of a problem or challenge so they can manage it more effectively. Over time, this approach actually increases conflict between family members and potentially damages relationships.

Bullying and scapegoating are behaviors that use intimidation as a way of avoiding the core issues in a family business conflict. Identifying bullying and scapegoating when they occur and ensuring that the appropriate parties are held accountable for their actions are two essential elements in managing these behaviors. However, at least as important is the decision by a family to ensure that every party to a difficult situation is given the opportunity to express his or her perspective in a safe and supportive environment. Exhibit 2.5 offers a few more suggestions on how to minimize bullying and scapegoating.

EXHIBIT 2.5   How to Minimize Bullying and Scapegoating

1. Create a family business culture that encourages personal responsibility and accountability.
2. Label the dysfunctional behaviors when you see them.
3. Ensure that all parties have a voice in dispute resolution, regardless of how loud or strong their opinions may be.

SIBLING RIVALRY

The sibling partnership stage is widely regarded as the most challenging and intense of the family business life cycle. Some of the difficulties seen at this stage are a result of predictable business challenges; however, most challenges that siblings who are working together encounter are related to emotional or relationship issues, which are typically harder to confront and to address than business struggles.

Although parents may recoil at the thought that they are to blame for the less-than-perfect behavior of their children, it cannot be denied that the way children are raised as siblings will have a profound effect on how they relate to one another as adults. In addition, even though siblings are raised in a similar environment, it is worth remembering that there are distinct personality differences that further complicate sibling relationships. Siblings tend to differentiate from one another to find their own place in the family system. This adds to the diversity of styles and interests that can make getting to consensus and working as a team more challenging. In fact, there are many ways that siblings' upbringing or differences get manifested in a family business.

Sibling rivalry often begins as normal competitiveness with children vying for their parents' attention. In many families, competiveness is viewed as a valuable personal trait and a coping skill; in some of these families, parents may even nurture competitiveness between siblings with a goal of "strengthening their character." But this can be taken too far, and children may not learn to set limits on competiveness or may not learn corresponding skills of collaboration and cooperation.

Some parents pit their children against each other by constantly comparing one to the other or intentionally having them compete and then belittling the "loser." This may continue to happen even as their children become adults and become active in the family business—for example, "your sales numbers this quarter are a bit disappointing; why don't you talk to your brother so he can show you how a true professional works?" These same parents then wonder why their children are always at each other's throats.

In other families, the problem of fair versus equal comes up again. Parents may become overly concerned about treating their children equally and believe that to be fair, they must treat all their children the same; this can apply to parental attention, love, material gifts, television time, anything. Children then come to believe that everyone should always and invariably be treated equally. However, as children grow into adults, it becomes more and more difficult for parents to treat their children equally because, in fact, each person is different. Parents and children may become so concerned with equality that they monitor what each receives from the others, and this encourages a self-orientation and increases competitiveness in the family. True equality in a family, however, comes from understanding, integrating, and appreciating individual differences, not from denying differences.

Imagine how much more complex sibling rivalry becomes when families share business interests: how early experiences of competiveness, self-orientation, and avoidance of conflict may readily lead to sibling conflicts around money, roles in the business, power, and authority. There is little doubt that childhood experiences shape views of one another and affect the ability to trust each other. This is why early sibling rivalry can intrude on subsequent efforts to work together. Moreover, siblings who work together and are obvious rivals run the risk that someone (such as a nonfamily employee) may pit siblings against one another.

Encourage your children—at every age, from the time they're very young to when they're adults who are working in the family business—to define and appreciate their own individual areas of competence and expertise. Celebrate the varied skills and interests of your children. Avoid the temptation to compare them to each other, but appreciate each child's unique gifts without comparison to siblings. While it can feel harmless and natural to describe one child as the "funny one" and another as the "smart one," be mindful that your children hang on your every word, and you can label and limit them from a very young age. In addition, while you should certainly give constructive feedback and acknowledge when your children are not measuring up, never mock or belittle your children—neither when they're small nor as adults.

Any parent who has more than one child learns very quickly the power of nature and nurture. Our children come into this world with distinct personalities, and although raised in the same house, they will experience their shared history quite differently from each other. Having said that, the context of their upbringing and shared history—especially around the

business—will leave a lasting impression and shape their perception of the business, one another, and their willingness to
work together as a family. While working to build a strong and
effective sibling team can be a challenge (for both the parents
and the siblings themselves), it is very worthwhile. Many sibling
groups thrive while working together and find real joy in deep-
ening their bonds with one another through the challenge and
excitement of shared business management and/or oversight. As
a parent, you have the opportunity and responsibility to set the
stage for strong sibling relations between your children, so make
the effort to do it right!

Encourage your children to solve their own problems and
even work together on projects from as early an age as possible.
When your children are young and arguing, unless bodily harm is
involved or imminent, resist the urge to get involved. When your
children run to you to complain about their siblings, offer them
empathy for their distress, but send them back to resolve the issue
with their siblings without your involvement. The sooner siblings
get used to relating to one another without the interference of
parents, the stronger their bond will be.

This approach is also important with adult children. As mentioned in the discussion of triangulation, your adult children may
still be turning to you to run interference or mediate, but you
should resist the temptation to get involved (even as a sounding board) and gently direct your adult children to communicate
directly with each other rather than with you.

Likewise, if you were raised in a very competitive house-
hold, think about how that experience might be affecting your

relationship with *your* siblings today and what steps you can take to develop a more collaborative working relationship with them. Admittedly, it can be hard to collaborate with a person with whom you have always been competing; therefore, it may be worthwhile to talk with your siblings about how each remembers these facets of your upbringing. Do not be surprised if each remembers the stories a little differently—memory is imperfect, and the point is to build mutual understanding, not to determine the "facts" or to bash your parents. You want to build empathy and understanding between yourself and your siblings and work together to acknowledge how this history may sometimes get in your way today.

While some parents may be very controlling of the business and not ready to give up a lot of authority, find ways to work with your siblings on special projects and on planning for the future. Work with your siblings to plan a family vacation or retreat or make a proposal to your parents about philanthropic pursuits for the family. Although your parents may not be ready to turn over the business decision-making reins to you anytime soon, as a sibling team, you can still work on such issues as determining the code of conduct you will use to govern your relationships. You can determine your decision-making process and even set a shared vision for the future of the business. If there are some siblings who work in the business and others who do not, it is particularly important (and impressive) if you can do some of this team building and decision making with all. Exhibit 2.6 provides suggestions on how to minimize the negative effects of sibling rivalry.

EXHIBIT 2.6   How to Minimize the Negative Effects of Sibling Rivalry

1. Clearly differentiate between ownership and management roles.

2. Keep siblings who are not working in the business informed and up-to-date.

3. Take time to put updated structures and policies in place well *before* they are needed. Work together to create clear, appropriate, proactive policies that manage sibling expectations about authority, compensation, and interactions with each other.

4. Devise clear and transparent methods for future compensation of family members working in the business.

5. Decide and agree together on how day-to-day management decisions will be made.

6. Identify and create governance structures that adequately support the business.

7. Use outside boards of directors who do not share the family history of competition and who can provide input that is viewed as objective and impartial.

8. Meet with your family on a regular basis to establish healthy communication. Make time for family meetings where *all* stakeholders build knowledge about the enterprise and develop stronger bonds with each other. Work together to create a family code of conduct for these meetings.

continued

9. Build a clearly shared sense of purpose for both business and the family.

10. Learn to build effective strategic plans that help determine paths for growth while also maintaining the core culture of the business.

11. Complete estate plans and make them known to family members. Remember: generosity in sharing information builds trust; secrecy destroys it.

12. Together devise liquidity and exit plans.

13. Spend time together *away* from the business as siblings and cousins.

14. Develop common interests with your siblings outside of the business.

15. Visit other sibling businesses together; learn from others' successes and mistakes (and do the same for other family businesses).

16. Keep your sibling rivalry to yourselves; airing tensions publicly hurts both the family and the business.

OPPORTUNITY AND PRIVILEGE

Another dilemma for business families lies in differing lifestyles and attitudes about money. Obviously, if the business is very successful, the lifestyles of family members will be affected in positive ways, particularly in terms of a broader set of opportunities in education, living standards, and recreation options.

Different people—even within the same family—have different ideas about how they want to live, and many families express their desire to prevent children from developing a sense of entitlement. There is good reason for this, because most family businesses proudly work to retain the founder's values of working hard, living within one's means, and expressing humility. But in subsequent generations, family members may have different ideas about how to uphold those values, creating dilemmas for individuals and their families. For example, one family member may want a larger house in a better neighborhood, another may want the family to travel to more exotic places, another may want to send the children to the most expensive schools. While there is nothing wrong or inappropriate about these opportunities, disagreements and conflicts about how money is spent and how the family acknowledges and upholds the family's values in practical ways can present a challenge.

An attitude of entitlement is usually evident when rewards are expected that are not commensurate with effort or ability invested. Parents who sacrificed much to build a business may be tempted to use money to replace attention they have been unable to offer, or they may wish simply to provide children and grandchildren with resources the parents or grandparents never dreamed of having. Some parents may try to compensate for inattention with endless praise for the smallest accomplishments. The result may be children with an overinflated sense of their own importance and a poor work ethic. Excessive praise and attention can also lead to feelings of jealousy or resentment between siblings and cousins when their parents' attitudes toward what is acceptable or deserved differs significantly from one family branch to the next.

People tend to not talk about money, but encouraging families to be more open about financial matters, especially in terms of how they fit in with the family vision and values, can be a productive conversation. A well-managed family business has a clear family vision and a clear business vision that includes a certain transparency about its financial matters, so that each family member knows (generally) what the others are doing. That's not to say every detail needs to be shared, but greater transparency and sharing of information will help decrease tension and conflict in the present while setting a healthy precedent for future generations. A helpful family vision is clear about some general guidelines as to how family members should live their lives and how individual and family charitable giving or philanthropy should be conducted. The most effective family vision is one that is balanced with the realization that as families grow, individual branches deserve respect for diversity and individual choices.

Making sure the next generation clearly understands the business and what it takes to work in any given aspect of it is key to appropriately limiting the dilemmas that can accompany financial success. While parents may not want to burden their children with work stress and worries, senior generations can ensure that children and grandchildren understand how much work goes into building a business. It is critical that they realize that it takes a whole team—not only the owners—to make things happen and to be successful. The contributions of key employees, the importance of teamwork, and the fragile nature of reputation should all be emphasized.

A business is actually an excellent platform for imbuing children with many valuable life lessons that will serve them well in their journey to be positive and contributing members of society, whether they have an active role in the business in the future or not. Children should not be sheltered from hard work or hard choices.

Family members in the next generation should take honest stock of their work ethic and their willingness to make sacrifices for the common good of the family and business. Whereas parents may have had the luxury of making decisions on their own, the next generation must be able to compromise or engage in give-and-take. If one or all are not able to make sacrifices for the good of the whole, ongoing joint ownership and/or management of a business may not be successful.

Next-generation family members should acknowledge when they need help and go out of their way to recognize the efforts and contributions of others (siblings and other key players in the business). They need to take responsibility for the hard choices of grown-up life or recognize that they cannot hope to be successful owners of a shared business.

Chapter 3

Guidelines for Dealing with Dilemmas That Lead to Conflict

CHECK YOUR ASSUMPTIONS

Experts in the behavioral sciences understand that we humans tend to fill in the blanks when we don't have all the facts, by making assumptions about individuals, groups, and circumstances. Part of the problem in relying on our assumptions to make decisions is that if the underlying information and the beliefs based on that information are incorrect, then the decisions will most likely not be wise or durable ones.

> Learning to identify your own assumptions is important because conflicts can be fueled when those assumptions limit growth and affect business decisions and relationships.

Understanding your own biases and assumptions is important for any relationship to thrive. This is particularly challenging for families in business together. For most of us, it is easier to hold assumptions—sometimes even unconsciously—and to prematurely come to conclusions about others' motives without even thinking about checking out the accuracy of those assumptions. In fact, studies have shown that people prefer to stick to their assumptions about other people or situations rather than engaging in an effort to more deeply understand a different point of view. That's not surprising, and this effect is magnified by the fact that real differences may not be adequately talked about in business families who strive to avoid conflict at any cost. This opens the door to significant misunderstandings of individual differences and to escalating conflict. It also leaves individual assumptions about those differences unchallenged and free to become "well-known facts," as opposed to *strongly held opinions*, leading to qualitative differences in decisions that are made based on those notions. Spending time to gain insight into how a belief or action may have developed is valuable in the process of learning to manage conflicts more effectively.

These assumptions about people and organizations can eventually become a part of our beliefs and ultimately inform our decisions. The challenge is first to recognize one's own assumptions clearly enough to honestly examine how they line up with factual information versus emotions or beliefs.

For example, the third-generation CEO of a successful auto parts manufacturing company proudly recruited all three of his adult sons to come work in the business. His plan had been for them to work as a leadership team, and it seemed to him to have taken hold beautifully: each of them settled into key roles managing the family business, and the business continued to thrive under this new leadership configuration.

Dad's plan was lovingly devised, based on the fact that his children got along well, had successfully completed business degrees from prestigious universities, and had spent at least one year each working successfully in businesses other than the family firm. Yet, none of these members of the fourth generation seemed to be completely satisfied in those jobs; in fact, all three had not been clear about what they really wanted to do with their careers and had actually begun the process of exploring other career paths when their father invited them "home" to work in the family business. Dad thought that coming back to work in the family company was the obvious and perfect plan for all three kids and would simultaneously allow him the time and energy to start winding down into semiretirement.

Ten months into this arrangement, the sons' mother began to notice that her children and their young families weren't spending much time together outside of work. When she pressed each of them about what she was observing, they all assured her everyone was just too busy and that they saw plenty of each other at work. Four months after that, dad himself began to notice less interaction among them at work outside of routine management meetings.

Although none of his children were willing to admit it, their relationships with each other had deteriorated as stark differences emerged around their individual management skill levels and styles. This in turn led to an undercurrent of conflict and avoidance that was beginning to become obvious even to employees. Unbeknownst to each other, each of the three children was considering exercising buy/sell agreements and leaving the family business.

Dad and each of his children had made key decisions based on their assumptions and beliefs about each other, the business, and the future. Among the assumptions on which the father had based his succession plan was the belief that each of his sons would be happiest working in the family business. After all, it had been a dream come true for him when he stepped in to work alongside his father and grandfather; moreover, the business had provided great opportunities for his family and the community both economically and socially. In addition, clearly none of his sons liked what he had been doing prior to joining the family business, and besides, "they'd always loved working together on projects as kids."

Similarly, each of the sons had his own assumptions, starting with the belief that each needed to physically work in the business in order to be a successful owner of the firm. They also tacitly colluded with one another to not disappoint their father by saying no to him when he invited them to come work in the family firm, especially when he had made them such a generous offer, believing that to do so would be too disappointing to their dad and disrespectful of the many years of hard work their grandfather and great-grandfather had poured into building such a successful business.

While it may seem clear in this scenario that a logical step would have been to double-check the data or facts that may have supported or debunked these notions, this isn't always an easy conversation to have or to even think about initiating. If the father had taken the time to genuinely inquire into each of his children's level of desire to come work in the firm, he might have learned that bringing in the three of them as a team wasn't the best approach. In turn, if the children had checked their beliefs that not communicating clearly with their dad would somehow spare his feelings, they could also have produced a different outcome and might even have been surprised about his level of positive support in helping them find what they really wanted to be doing.

A critical first step is *taking the time* to understand each family member's unique interpretation of original data or events, with a specific emphasis on how certain assumptions may have informed each person's beliefs and affected actions based on those beliefs. Each person can then seek to understand similar processes that other family members may have followed to reach their conclusions.

Exhibit 3.1 provides ten questions to ask yourself to assess your own conflict management skills.

EXHIBIT 3.1   Assessing Your Conflict Management Skills: Ten Reflection Questions

1. Can I identify any assumptions I have been holding that may be coloring my interpretation of events and conclusions I have drawn?
2. Have I made time to check out my own interpretation of information or events with other family members?

continued

3. Have I made time to talk with other family members about those assumptions while working toward a better understanding?

4. How might I develop a more open-minded approach to simply better understand other family members' interpretation of the same data or events?

5. Can I separate my feelings from what the other person may have intended?

6. Which of my own "buttons" is being pushed? Might I be reacting to personality differences or to events in the distant past?

7. Is my reaction in proportion to the conflict?

8. How might my attitude toward the problem or the person be influencing my perception?

9. How have I specifically contributed to the problem?

10. What specific actions can I take to build trust between us?

PRACTICE ACTIVE LISTENING

Conflict in the family business can often be attributed to poor communication: people misunderstand one another, or they ascribe motives to each other that might not actually be there, or they allow historical hurts and emotions to blow simple disagreements out of proportion. Most of the time, the key to resolving conflict lies in communicating well and arriving at mutually agreed-upon courses of action.

At its very heart, good communication means *good listening*, but far too often people are just not good listeners:

◆ They interrupt each other.

◆ They prepare a response to another's communication even before that person has had a chance to finish what he or she meant to say.

◆ They mistakenly assume that they understand each other when they really *misunderstand* each other.

In his book *The 7 Habits of Highly Effective People*, Stephen Covey wrote, "Seek first to understand, then to be understood."[1] Listening to others in order to understand their points of view not only produces better relationships, it also increases the likelihood of your being understood by the other parties.

Listening well is critical to effective communication because often when people are in conflict, each party thinks that what the other is saying doesn't make sense or is irrational. For example, if a family member complains about "always being treated unfairly," one of the most unhelpful responses might be "that's ridiculous! I've gone out of my way to treat you fairly for the past 25 years!" Obviously, that's not a good way to start a conversation about differences in perspectives and real-life experiences, but it does highlight those differences in a very clear way. The fact that someone else's feeling doesn't make sense to *you* doesn't mean it isn't very real to *that person*, because *perception*

---

[1] Stephen R. Covey. *The 7 Habits of Highly Effective People* (New York: Free Press, 2004), ch. 5.

is reality. Understanding this and responding with this in mind can go a long way toward managing long-standing tensions by understanding how that feeling and experience has developed and made sense to that family member. Once you have some understanding of why he or she feels this way, then you can begin to work out solutions with each other.

It is also important to note that really, truly understanding another person does NOT mean that you agree with everything said. Too often, people get caught up in thinking that understanding another person means agreeing with him or her.

Exhibit 3.2 offers guidelines on how to listen well.

EXHIBIT 3.2   Steps for Listening Well

Active Listening refers to a set of behaviors that enhance mutual understanding, ensure good listening, and encourage others to communicate effectively:

1. Be respectful and interested.
2. To listen without being defensive, assume that what is being said is true for the person saying it, whether or not you agree—then you must decide how and why it is true for that person.
3. Paraphrase or mirror what is being said: "So what you're saying is..." or "Let me see if I understand..." or the like.
4. After paraphrasing ask for feedback: "Is that accurate?"

5. Ask probing questions using "how," "where," "when," and "what." For example, "When do you feel this? It would help me if you gave me an example of the last time this occurred." Or "What did I do that made you think of that?" Don't give your opinions.

6. When the speaker is finished, summarize what you heard.

7. Accept the speaker's message: "I understand that you would feel _____ because _____." Or "It makes sense that you would think _____ because _____."

Remember, you don't need to *agree* in order to *understand*!

ENSURE CLEAR AND FAIR PROCESSES

Another fundamental element in managing conflict is to ensure that adequate, widely agreed-upon processes are in place for making decisions, both in the present and for the future. Most decisions about business or family matters are arrived at with relatively little difficulty, but if the process by which decisions are made is viewed as fair, there is a much greater chance that those decisions will be sustainable and effective, even if some individuals are not 100 percent in agreement: if the process agreed on is followed and viewed as fair, then the decision will be a durable one, and the quality of family relationships will be preserved. In developing clear processes for decision making, there are several strategies to consider.

Empowering responsible management to act on behalf of the family and the business is a key to future success, yet other decisions need to be made by the CEO and still others by the family. Determining when decisions can be made by nonfamily managers or by family leaders and when to include other family owners who are not working in the business can be a daunting task.

Because conflicts often tend to come up around the appropriate inclusion of other owners (those who may be overseeing key elements of the business and those who may be less involved but owners nevertheless), an important first step to preventing conflict before it starts is to create a framework that outlines what kind of decisions need to be brought before which family owners, with a view toward minimizing all surprises. In best-case scenarios, all family members know the issues and are informed about the call for a decision far in advance of that decision being made. Setting up agreements to this effect can become an important element of family bylaws or even policies to be included in a family constitution or family charter that may contain all the family's written agreements.

Other considerations in ensuring a clear and fair process include thinking together about how to clarify personal agendas and minimize potential conflicts of interest before a decision must be made and providing ample time for family members to prepare their thoughts, express their views, and ask questions, all in an unrushed environment. This means creating the time, space, and expectation that this approach will always precede those critical family decisions. Decisions that feel rushed almost always feel unfair.

But these processes don't guarantee complete agreement in every case. Valuing and working toward consensus, even when there remains disagreement, can provide an environment that encourages family members to address their concerns in a genuine effort to find a best-case solution together. Bringing in an objective outsider to help facilitate these kinds of decisions is another effective strategy, as is reviewing the decision one more time before it is implemented. In this important review, all discuss their views of the agreed-upon process and agree to review the results of the decision later if necessary. Exhibit 3.3 describes the key elements of a fair process.

UTILIZE STRUCTURE

Another fundamental element in managing conflict well is creating structures and a *system of governance* that support your family's intentions going forward and that provide opportunities for all family members (whether or not they're working in the family business) to contribute in some way. For example, a family might create a *family council*, or a *philanthropy committee*, or a *social committee*. In addition, the family may create family wide policies, such as a code of conduct, a compensation policy, and/or a family employment policy.

These structures and policies are important because business families typically do things almost reactively, or off-the-cuff, instead of more formally (the way nonfamily businesses usually have policies and procedures already in place).

EXHIBIT **3.3**   Key Elements to Ensuring a Fair Process[2]

1. *No surprises*: Everyone knows the issues and is informed about the call to decision beforehand.

2. *No conflicts of interest*: Personal interests and agendas are revealed beforehand. No hidden agendas.

3. *No rush*: Everyone feels that they have had time to prepare and time to present their views.

4. *Sincere care*: Each participant feels respected and heard.

5. *Mutual commitment and good faith*: Genuine effort is made to find a win-win solution, and no effort put into gaining an unfair advantage.

6. *Belief in the viability of consensus*: The goal is to arrive at an agreed-upon plan of action while acknowledging there may be differing points of view.

7. *Objective outsiders*: If outsiders are involved, independent directors or family facilitators represent the interests of everyone, not just some and not special interests.

8. *Postdecision review*: Everyone discusses his or her views of the process and agrees to review the results of the decision later if necessary. Until then, all parties will publicly agree on the outcome despite potentially differing views.

---

[2] This information is adapted from material provided by John Ward, cofounder of the Family Business Consulting Group, Inc.

And as mentioned earlier, that reactivity is often at the root of many conflicts. Therefore, one benefit of having a system of governance is that it introduces more thoughtfulness regarding key decisions, and it helps manage expectations—which is especially important because *mismanaged expectations are often the source of conflict.* The process of developing these governance structures can in itself help solidify family cohesion. If the family works together to successfully create agreements that have broad acceptance, members have an increased sense of accomplishment and a clearer, widely shared vision for themselves and for the business.

For example, as alluded to in chapter 2 in a discussion of compensation, some family members might believe that family members should receive high compensation by virtue of family membership; other family members might think that family should be paid only at levels that are customary for a particular position in a specific industry; different expectations of this sort very often are at the heart of conflict. When families create policies about compensation and work together to arrive at an agreement, the resulting document can ultimately help manage expectations, and the experience of working together to arrive at a consensus regarding an important issue can strengthen family bonds.

Of course, it's easier to simply say you're going to create policies; keep in mind that you actually have to *do* it. That process might involve the following steps:

- assembling the appropriate family members together in one place at a specific time,
- discussing matters calmly,

- actively listening to each other, and finally
- refraining from acting impulsively when deciding what your family business policies are going to be.

These family policies don't need to be anywhere near as extensive as the policy manuals one might find in a Fortune 500 company. In fact, the most elegant and most effective policies are usually very simple. Don't get so caught up in creating structures and policies that you end up spending all your time and energy in setting policies for every possible situation; in that case, you may be making things too complex without realistically setting an intention to follow the policies that you create. Moreover, as noted earlier, it is often not the policy itself that is of greatest value but the experience of the family working together to create a positive outcome.

Some family members might believe that they don't need to create policies because they may feel, "we're not that big a business that we need to have formal policies for the way we do things." A policy doesn't need to be lengthy or complicated; however, every family business should have a few simple guidelines that most family members agree with and that bring clarity to family and business. Your policies should provide a straightforward road map, so when questions come up in the future, you'll have a head start in knowing how your family wants to handle them.

Your policies should be written down; that's absolutely critical. That doesn't mean that you need to create a policy manual (although that might help), but you should have a record that you can turn to so that if there's a question or disagreement in the future, your family has a reference point in a written guideline and can say, "Back in 20xx, we actually decided together that here are the three steps that should be followed."

Policies themselves can sometimes be a source of conflict. For example, a family might have a policy stating that every family member should work outside the family business for at least three years. If the family then allows someone to join the family business after working outside for only two years, the policy hasn't been followed and that situation can now be a source of conflict. Occasionally, this happens because policies created at an earlier time no longer make sense in the present economy and competitive environment. In this sense, policies should be viewed as living documents that are revised and reviewed as necessary and with some regularity.

Finally, if a family is arguing about a policy, the conflict may be deeper than the policy itself, so the policy can at least point to what's really happening. Exhibit 3.4 offers suggestions for establishing policies, structures, and strategies.

EXHIBIT 3.4   Establishing Policies and Structures That Benefit Business and Family

- Talk openly with family members about the advantages of adding structure to family and business.
- Start by identifying policies to which everyone can agree. Move to more challenging policies later.

continued

- ◆ Conduct family meetings that are specifically intended to address the need for policies and structures.
- ◆ Consider creating a family constitution or family charter that will constitute a hard copy of the policies you create.
- ◆ A family employment policy is one policy that most business families should have. Be clear and deliberate about how newly added family members are incorporated into the family, what preparations are necessary, and to what extent they might be involved in the business.
- ◆ Other useful policies might include a distribution policy, a family code of conduct, and a policy for terminating family employment.

ARE YOU BUSINESS FIRST OR FAMILY FIRST?

Another element in preventing or reducing conflict is to know where your family stands on certain basic principles in the big picture of balancing family and business. As more family members from new generations begin to work in the business or assume ownership and receive financial or other benefits, the business will naturally become more complex. At the same time, as more people are involved, there's more opportunity for conflict among family members who are trying to understand how to stay engaged with both the business and the family.

One way of understanding how your family business fits into the big picture is by imagining a continuum with one end marked by business families who put *family* first. These families believe their interpersonal relationships are paramount, even if that means the business suffers in some way. At the other end of this continuum are business families who put *business* first; these families operate with a keen eye on the bottom line, even if that means that some family relationships may suffer or be damaged in the process of ensuring that the business is financially successful.

At the extreme, family members in a family business that is *family first* believe that in the event of business challenges that are seriously damaging to family relationships, then the family would rather sell the business than let it hurt those interpersonal relationships. In contrast, in a family business that is *business first*, family members believe that the business is of paramount importance because without the business, the family wouldn't survive. Where business is valued over family, family members who are chronically dissatisfied with the way the business is being managed or who are consistently at the heart of conflict that affects success of the business are more likely to be helped to exit in order to keep the business intact and thriving. In other words, a family that puts business first would rather risk family harmony than risk business success.

The important consideration here is understanding the family's priorities on this family first/business first continuum, so as to properly manage and guide family expectations in the long term. When families clarify their priorities in this manner, they can then create policies that support and guide decision making based on those priorities. For example, a family that puts family first might work to create jobs for qualified family members, but one that puts business first is more likely to hire only the best person for an open position, whether or not that person is a family member.

> The availability of a structured approach to renewal and reconciliation can help a family move out of negative patterns and toward more normalized relationships.

SMALL SHIFTS THAT MAKE A DIFFERENCE

Stay Calm

Sometimes, families have been in conflict over a particular issue for such an extended period of time that whenever the issue comes up the conversation quickly gets heated to the point where family members can't even have a calm discussion about it anymore.

While continually ignoring conflict may have negative consequences, there are instances when shifting the focus away from negativity also changes the tone in communication between family members, allowing breathing space while reminding family members of the positive aspects of the family and the business. Maybe the business had a very profitable quarter or landed a significant new client. Perhaps a grandchild earned an academic award in school. By changing the subject to something positive and appreciated by all family members, the temperature in the room can be shifted to help reengage everyone in a more civil conversation. In this case, families are not avoiding conflict but restoring a sense of positive regard.

In fact, staying calm sets a good tone for everybody involved. There's considerable research that emotions are contagious, so someone who is angry is likely to elicit an angry response from others. Neurobiological researchers of mirror neurons have found that when these neurons are stimulated, they arouse emotions that are similar to the emotions being observed in someone else.

Regulate Your Own Tension

Part of regulating a relationship in which there are tensions is to regulate yourself. If you're able to stay calm, you help others stay calm too. The first step in trying to resolve or manage conflict is to manage your own emotions.

Of course, sometimes managing your own emotions is easier said than done, but working to *be aware of your own reactivity* is an important first step. Giving additional thought to *what outcomes are most desirable* in a situation sets a frame of reference and goal that decreases the likelihood that emotion will drive the situation.

Remember the old saying that *the only person you can change is yourself.* By taking personal responsibility for managing the emotional atmosphere, family members can maintain appropriate control over their own emotional reactions while helping to provide an environment that is less volatile and more respectful to others.

Strive to Be Inclusive

Dissatisfactions in family businesses often develop when some people are not included in planning or family governance. When family members feel they don't have a voice in important matters, they may voice their feelings and opinions in ways that are not constructive—or they may opt out of family relationships completely.

This often happens when families exclude in-laws from their planning, from decision making, and from family meetings. As a result, in-laws may develop negative views toward the business and toward the family, and this will increase the potential for conflicts to emerge in their generation that may then impact generations to follow. Therefore, it's helpful to have agreed-upon guiding principles that clearly outline the family's definition of who is included in various family matters and why.

Understand and Accept Differences and Diversity

Even though they are members of the same family system, fundamental differences in personality and perspective often abound among parents, siblings, and cousins. This is particularly true when children, in-laws, and geographical distance are introduced to the family. Failing to understand basic differences and how they affect perspective or viewing differences as wrong or "unnatural" can open the door to escalating tensions and full-blown conflicts. For example, one sibling may thrive on competition, whereas his brother is perhaps skilled at bringing people together to collaborate. Or one sibling tends to approach challenges head-on, tackling problems and solving them quickly, whereas her brother tends to approach issues quietly and thoughtfully, making a decision only after every aspect and potential impact have been carefully considered. Or an adult child may value "green" initiatives, even at the cost of profits to the business, while her parent could not imagine making that trade-off. These differences do not need to be disruptive or destructive, provided that the differing perspectives are understood and respected and that efforts are made to ensure that all parties have a voice in decision making and that a fair process is followed.

Manage Meetings Effectively

Establishing ground rules for family meetings ensures that meetings stay on track and are a productive and worthwhile use of everyone's time. Every family can develop its own ground rules to meet its specific needs, but all ground rules should include appropriate guidelines to provide structure and consistency. The time, place, topics to be discussed, and the attention and focus of everyone involved are all critical to ensuring successful meetings.

Set a specific agenda for your meeting that lists the topics or issues that need to be discussed and distribute the agenda to all participants beforehand. Set a time frame for the meeting, and stick to it: beginning and ending the meeting on time is critically important. Conduct your meeting in a comfortable and appropriate location. Ask support people not to interrupt anyone in the meeting and ask everyone who is attending to turn off their cell phones, etc., so that they can truly focus on the purpose of the meeting.

Developing healthy communication behaviors and habits will go a long way toward limiting the impact of dilemmas and containing conflict. Learn to listen respectfully to each person and don't interrupt others. Remember that the best way to have someone listen to you is to listen to the other person—you will have your turn to express your point of view. Make sure that everyone has an opportunity to speak.

Keep in mind that it is quite feasible to work to understand what someone is saying without agreeing with that person; sometimes families struggle over agreement and disagreement without establishing mutual understanding first. Don't fall into that trap; simply try to understand what others are saying before deciding or judging their ideas.

One way to accomplish this is to ask the speaker to repeat what was just said for clarification and better understanding. This ensures that everyone is paying attention to the discussion. Then, summarize what has been said for verification. This helps put everyone "on the same page" in terms of understanding and can help the speaker feel heard and understood. This process will help to ensure that the discussion stays focused on the topics and issues at hand rather than on the personality of anyone at the meeting.

Allow time for each person to present his or her case and be sure to take turns so that everyone has an opportunity to speak. Don't let others criticize or even comment on a person's opinion until everyone has spoken at least once. Keep track of the various opinions on a flip chart, so all ideas can be reviewed before making a decision. Make sure that there is adequate time to get all the facts on the table and that questions have been vetted and clarified before making a decision.

Remember that emotions are contagious, so it is important to stay calm, relaxed, and focused. If the discussion begins to get heated, take a short break. Serving refreshments also helps sustain a mood of calm participation, rather than an adversarial situation.

It may also be helpful to establish a goal of disagreeing in private but not in front of others. Conduct meetings behind closed doors, and when the meeting is over, leave disagreements until your next meeting.

EXHIBIT 3.5   **Eight Steps to Better Communication**

1. **Listen** not only to the words but also to the meaning behind them.
2. **Seek** understanding rather than victory.
3. **Don't** let disagreements fester.
4. **Create** a "safe" environment for discussion—suspend judgment.
5. **Accept** others' rights to their feelings and conclusions.
6. **Complain** directly—not through a third party.
7. **Put the past behind you**—don't base your reactions on childhood.
8. **Avoid certainty**—conclusive statements shut off discussion, such as "That will never work" or "We tried that already."

Keep in mind that consensus means "we have agreed to follow a course of action." It does not mean that all members of the group must see things the same way, but once you've decided on that course of action, everyone must support it 100 percent even if that course wasn't the one someone would have chosen on his or her own.

If you think the meeting is likely to be contentious, use a facilitator who is experienced in conducting family meetings. Make sure that the facilitator will keep the meeting focused on the agenda, will understand the impact of psychological and family dynamics, and will work to reduce the emotional reactivity of the participants. Having an outsider present can help everyone stay calm and discuss the issues rather than past grievances. Keep track of issues that have been resolved and of matters that need continued attention. Finally, set up your next meeting before ending this one.

Exhibit 3.5 above sums up the suggestions for better communication we've covered in this chapter, and Exhibit 3.6 lists the ground rules for meetings.

EXHIBIT 3.6   Ground Rules for Family Meetings

1. **Structure the meeting**: Set a clear time and place, distribute an agenda of topics to cover, and request full attention without interruptions.
2. **Listen well**: Make sure everyone has a chance to talk and don't interrupt each other.
3. **Seek first to understand**: Remember that understanding someone doesn't imply that you agree with that person's point of view.

4. **Use active listening skills**: Encourage participants to sum up what others have said to ensure that everyone really hears other people's points of view.

5. **Stay calm**: Take a break if the discussion becomes heated and serve refreshments to lighten the atmosphere.

6. **Focus on issues**: Don't dwell on personalities, and don't rehash past grievances.

7. **Use brainstorming techniques**: Make sure everyone has a chance to speak and don't interrupt, censure, or criticize what others say.

8. **Respect privacy**: Don't air private disagreements in public.

9. **Seek consensus**: Even if everyone doesn't agree, everyone must abide by the decisions made at family meetings.

10. **Use facilitation**: Consider bringing in an outside facilitator to help everyone stay focused on the issues and to help keep heated emotions from clouding discussion.

11. **Follow up**: Clarify what actions need to be taken and by whom as a result of this meeting and set up the next meeting.

Chapter 4

Create a Legacy for Future Generations

KEEPING DILEMMAS, TENSIONS, AND CONFLICTS IN CHECK

One of the most important exercises in which a business family can engage is identifying, articulating, and clarifying its core vision and mission—both for the family and the business. Typically, this is part of the business strategic planning processes, but it is also important from the standpoint of ensuring that the vision and mission are clear and owned by all family members and stakeholders. This process is critical in making important business decisions and decisions regarding the roles and responsibilities of family members. But it is also an important step for effectively preventing future conflicts in the family.

On the business side, a clearly thought out and articulated vision and mission will help guide the family's succession planning and implementation for the next generation. That might include a picture of the future that empowers each member of the next-generation management team to lead and operate specific divisions or departments, with team meetings to address decisions affecting the enterprise as a whole. This vision could include an explicit desire for individual team members to

- be held to common, clearly articulated, and specific evaluation processes,
- operate as a team, as opposed to being led by an individual or a separate coalition branch, and
- avoid the "ruler" mentality of one family member dominating those processes.

On the other hand, the shared mission and vision that the family articulates for itself will provide a clear picture of how family members want to interact with each other, with employees, and with the broader community. The shared mission and vision provide guidance for family philanthropy or the establishment of a family foundation. The point is that families should work to *not* leave these processes to chance and to ground them solidly in guidelines that grow out of the family's mission and vision.

This also requires that families are aware when their mission and/or vision may have shifted a bit and are prepared to make changes together accordingly. Dad's vision of the company when he started it—from daily operations to executive decision making to giving back to the community—will have evolved by the time he is ready to transition to the next generation. For example, the daily "standup" meetings with managers in the hallway when the company had 50 employees will likely not be as efficient a way to meet and communicate by the time the next generation takes over leadership and the enterprise has grown to more than 1,000 employees.

Some families resist this kind of realignment of vision and mission caused by changes to the enterprise because the original business operations supported one of the family's core values about treating nonfamily managers "like family" and building a family "feel" even among employees working on the shop floor. Family members may say, "If we become that 'professional,' we'll lose one of the reasons why we are in business in the first place."

This is not a small issue for some families in that it demands that the family members revisit their common understanding of the company's mission and vision in which difficult questions will need to be addressed:

- How large of an enterprise do we want to own and manage?
- Do we view the close "family feel" of our father's business as core to how we do business? If so, how are we going to maintain that culture while still growing the business?
- What do we need to do as owners and/or managers working in the business to better prepare ourselves to lead a growing business?
- How do we see ourselves giving back to the immediate community under the current circumstances?
- How might that need to shift with future growth (or decline)?

Of course, any changes in the business will require this level of clarity concerning family and enterprise mission and vision, including economic decline, which might mean that a family needs to revisit its shared picture of long-term retirement or distribution goals or its commitment to not lay off any employees during hard times—all based on the family's common mission

---

EXHIBIT 4.1   Align Vision and Mission to Manage Future Tensions

- Understand the founders' unique view of the business and the family.
- Work together to understand, clarify, and own your business's mission and vision.
- Develop a strategic plan and operating plan that support your family's mission and vision.
- Develop a plan to reassess these when change occurs (succession, economy, company growth/decline, etc.).
- Create a plan to engage all family stakeholders in this process for the future.

---

and vision of how the enterprise will be led and managed. This clarity is key to helping manage challenges, tensions, and conflicts that are (as we said at the beginning of this book) *predictable* but *not inevitable* in any family business.

Exhibit 4.1 presents an overview of the key points to keep in mind about the vision and mission of your family and your business to help you manage future tensions.

MINIMIZING DESTRUCTIVE ENTITLEMENT

In some families, the notion of what is historically perceived as fair or equal can also have an impact on the way current conflicts take shape. These conflicts most often arise from a *perceived injustice* in which one family member or an entire branch of a family feels there has been unfair or unjust treatment in past years or past generations. That sense of injustice can be very powerful, leading to resentments and grudges between family members or in subsequent generations in a way that not only interferes with family unity but also causes current conflict concerning the family enterprise. One result of this sort of unresolved conflict being carried over from the past is that current family members may believe that ignoring or mistreating those they believe to be associated with the original injustice is warranted.

In some individuals and families, this results in a perception of being entitled to mistreat or victimize others, hence the term "destructive entitlement." Whether or not these others were directly responsible for the original betrayal is irrelevant; so long as the others are related to the original perpetrator, they are held responsible for the historical abuses, and legacies of unfair treatment may be sustained through stories that are passed on from one generation to the next.

Destructive entitlement can perpetuate conflict in families based on individual perceptions of unfairness from the past, making the idea of collaboration or peace seem like a betrayal to family members who were initially hurt by unfair practices. This sets up a cycle of conflict, dilemmas, and tensions that are perpetuated over time. Because victims of unfair treatment in the past feel entitled to ignore or mistreat others in the present, they repeat hurtful behaviors resulting in more hurt feelings and leading to a dynamic of escalating victimization and victimhood.

In multigenerational family businesses, perceptions of fairness in the present may not be simply a function of current behavior—what may appear logically and currently fair may not be fair in a historical context. The stories around old injustices themselves may contribute to a general distrust in the family system and the business, which can have further challenging consequences for both.

Exhibit 4.2 offers some suggestions for dealing with destructive entitlement and perceived injustices.

EXHIBIT 4.2   Suggestions for Dealing with Destructive Entitlement

- ◆ Recognize the feelings you have about an old hurt or injustice in your family; initially, you might have a sense of justice or "righteousness" or a feeling of sadness and anger.
- ◆ Encourage respected family members and leaders to appeal to others to create a process of reconciliation, recognizing that most of them can see the need to break the destructive cycle.
- ◆ Acknowledge how you (and other family members) may be contributing to keeping past conflicts alive. Be specific about behaviors: are there family members with whom you refuse to speak?
- ◆ Acknowledge and accept responsibility for how historical injustices might have been perpetuated.
- ◆ Separate the instigators of the original offense from their descendants or extended family members.

- Appeal to those identified as perpetrators—or as related to perpetrators—to acknowledge the cycle of conflict and to request forgiveness.

- Find ways to move toward a sense of forgiveness, which does not mean saying the perceived injustice was okay.

- Understand that developing a sense of forgiveness will require more on the part of the victim than the perpetrator of the injustice, *but* understand as well that forgiveness brings greater benefit to victims than to perpetrators.

- Create opportunities for dialogue and open encounter between those who disagree.

- Create options for restitution if appropriate and called for.

- Bring in a skilled mediator for assistance, particularly if the cycle of destructive entitlement has resulted in lawsuits between family members.

BE AWARE OF HOW HISTORY REPEATS ITSELF

In some families, difficult tensions are managed by stopping communication altogether once a conflict or misunderstanding has reached a "last straw" point. It may seem like an immediate solution to feeling overwhelmed by negative emotion to just stop talking to each other and so the conflict doesn't have to stay visibly in play. Some people call this an *emotional cutoff.*

Emotional cutoffs may begin with a cycle of destructive entitlement and victimization. As noted earlier, this kind of conflict management "solution" can be prolonged and even handed down to subsequent generations. Once the breaking point is reached, the amount of hurt and sadness seemingly justifies the cutoff. The person or group in question is no longer included in family events, and there is no communication with that person or group. Without intervention and over time, this person or group may become virtually unknown in the family or known only by a reputation that may or may not reflect reality.

But histories of long-standing family conflict and cutoffs being repeated from one generation to the next don't justify the impacts on the extended family, particularly one associated with a successful enterprise. The problem with emotional cutoffs is that they don't solve anything and only produce an immediate but temporary sense of calm; this masks the discomfort caused by the conflict but does not address its underlying causes.

In fact, in many business families, the members of one generation are afraid that the difficulties they've had in their generation *will* be passed on to the next generation. Bad habits are not what most people want to leave to their children; fortunately, some people are aware that such habits may be transferred from one generation to the next and work to prevent it. Exhibit 4.3 offers a step-by-step process to help you manage conflicts more effectively.

Although taking a time-out is sometimes an effective strategy to regain some perspective in the heat of a conflict, it isn't an effective long-term strategy. Make time to invest in rebuilding trust with family members. Communicate clearly with them and emphasize your desire to do so and explain what specifically you would like to do

---

EXHIBIT 4.3   **Seven Steps to Aid in Managing Conflicts More Effectively in Family Businesses**

1. Identify where circumstances may be unintentionally fueling hard feelings.
2. Commit to keep meeting together socially.
3. Commit to regular family meetings regarding the enterprise.
4. Get a solid board of directors in place to help you make better decisions.
5. Identify policies to be created to avoid future problems as much as possible.
6. In leadership teams, make sure roles are spelled out and clear to everyone with accountability processes in place outside of the team.
7. Pay attention to your family's mission and vision, commit to making decisions based on them.

---

to make that happen. Get outside help from a counselor, clergy, or trusted advisor to have conversations and to agree together on goals for interacting and relating to each other in moving forward. Agree that not talking to each other is not a strategy worth pursuing.

DON'T HAND DOWN BAD HABITS

Most business owners would agree that some conflict is simply a part of running a business. But tensions within a family business are usually managed in the same way the family and its individual family members have done it for many years, and those patterns are established early as a part of a family's dynamics. This isn't necessarily a negative approach, but it is worth thinking about the legacy of ineffective conflict management patterns that might be handed down to future generations. These patterns are likely to become even less effective as the family grows and the business becomes more complex.

This is particularly true when a family's "native" patterns of managing tensions include unconscious habits that sometimes keep family members from fully making their thinking and rationale clear to those around them. This sort of incomplete reasoning represents one of the most likely group of patterns for managing tensions that could be handed down to future generations as a part of a family's culture, as the "way we do things."

These patterns can also play a major role in the way conflict is instigated, managed, maintained, or avoided. For example, some families may value protecting family members and preserving important relationships over airing tensions that would seem to disrupt that sense of protection. Other families may have an unspoken rule that says family members should not make mistakes, which results in a fear of being wrong and a possible resistance to admitting mistakes that have been made. Being aware of some of these ineffective patterns a family may use in managing tensions is important so family members can avoid handing them down to future generations.

Awareness of their use and power in a family can lead to opportunities to limit how many ineffective patterns are handed down to the next generation while developing more effective patterns for use in the family business today. Again, these are *ineffective* approaches to managing conflict, so these are habits you should try to break and *not* pass down to future generations:

1. *Amping Up*: Some people tend to become louder and more insistent when making a point, which diverts attention away from other perspectives or viable alternatives and eventually wears down everyone else until others just "opt out" and agree with the loudest opinion.

2. **Being Nice**: Some families use good manners and being pleasant in public as a way to avoid close examination of difficult decisions. In their minds, being nice is more important than being honest, and therefore healthy honesty isn't practiced.

3. **Don't Talk**: Most families have "undiscussables"—topics or actions that everyone understands are off-limits for public discussion or for discussion with other family members. The tacit buy-in into this unspoken rule means, for example, that although Uncle Joe drinks heavily during the evening cocktail hour and sometimes comes to work with a hangover, no one confronts him because "there will be hell to pay" afterward. So no one speaks up.

4. **Keeping the Peace (no matter what)**: Avoidance of conflict is an approach to tension management that at first glance seems to work really well. However, eventually, the conflict comes out in other ways that could damage the business and/or family members' relationships with each other.

5. ***Communicating Indirectly***: If someone talks to other family members about another's behavior (triangulating), the person who is triangulating doesn't have to deal with his or her own responsibility for decisions or behavior that may have contributed to the problems initially.

6. ***Barreling Through***: If some family member manages situations unilaterally and appears frantically busy enough, other family members who question that person's actions can't catch him or her long enough to ask about that person's rationale. Although this pattern maintains a semblance of control, it is most often driven by a fear of failure.

7. ***Saving Face (at all costs)***: Some people work hard to make sure no one gets upset or defensive (including themselves). On the surface, this routine looks like a nice way of interacting with others, but if it is overused, it blocks any opportunity to examine and improve decision making.

8. ***Blaming***: Someone who deflects responsibility onto someone else limits the conversation about his or her contribution to a negative outcome.

9. ***Intellectualizing***: If you don't have to address your feelings, not only do you protect yourself from discomfort, but you also keep the true range of your motives from becoming visible to yourself and others while maintaining an illusion of logical and sound thinking.

These patterns are usually so ingrained in family interactions that they are generally not recognized as anything more than "that's just the way our family operates." But they also rarely reflect the values espoused or desired by the business or embraced by the family. By becoming aware of ways family members use these patterns and then redirecting them, families can appropriately channel conflict, increase productivity in the business, and improve relationships among family members.

RECONCILE PAST INJUSTICES AND CUTOFFS

Business families have been connected to each other through generations of shared ownership. Over the course of a long shared history, it is likely that some past injustices have occurred, which could lead to dynamics of destructive entitlement and cycles of repetitive attempts to rebalance the scorecard (as discussed above). When these patterns take hold, they can keep a family from moving forward and can lead to escalating negative consequences for the family as well as for the business. A structured approach to renewal and reconciliation can help a family move out of negative patterns and toward more normalized relations. This can mean the difference between success and failure in implementing plans to sustain the family's enterprise for many generations.

Forgiveness is an essential part of that renewal and reconciliation, but these are processes rather than single acts. Forgiveness in a family that has been handicapped by perceptions of past injustice must be introduced, shaped, and integrated within an overall strategy in order for a family to move forward. Family members who wish to maintain some level of relationship or who want to experience more peace of mind are candidates for engaging in a process of forgiveness and reconciliation.

Consider the example in which a father had acquired a single apartment building in 1924 and continued to buy real estate until his company owned several apartment complexes, office buildings, commercial retail space, and a property management company. Dad and his wife placed real estate acquisitions in trusts for their five children. Dad advised his children to stick together and maintain their holdings as one enterprise; to reinforce his high-control philosophy, he gave voting stock to his three sons who were active in the business but gave only nonvoting stock to his two daughters.

The youngest of the children, a daughter, always wanted to join the business. After her father's passing, she did. She was a lawyer and soon made sweeping improvements to the property management division. Over time, as her contribution to the family enterprise continued to grow, the original distribution of voting and nonvoting stock among the five children became a source of strained relations between them. The brothers understood that their sisters were angry and felt like second-class family members. Nevertheless, they were clear on the value of tight control in an expanding family, and they refrained from discussing the injustice that had been unwittingly started by their father.

The sisters and their families attended family events but felt awkward; the reason for the awkwardness was not discussed. It was understood that the existing ownership arrangement was nonnegotiable, and no one wanted "to open Pandora's box." Tension escalated from time to time, however, usually playing out at family social functions.

Hope for improved family harmony was finally generated when a board member suggested that the family seek reconciliation for

the good of all. The youngest daughter and her sister were coun-
seled that they should not go into this process seeking retribution
or punishment, but rather seeking recognition that they had been
victims of an unintended consequence of their father's decision.

Different perceptions of a precipitating event can result
in different versions of "the truth," which are never calibrated
because most families lack a vehicle for communicating these
perceptions. As a result, past injustices endure.

In this family, individual sibling meetings culminated in a
single family meeting that began the family's healing. The siblings were advised to listen only. Through a structured communication process, they recounted how they first heard about
the stock split and the reasoning provided by their father, which
revealed that although the brothers had felt awkward in accepting the voting stock, they had not resisted when their father
provided it. The sisters heard their brothers acknowledge, without making excuses or justifications, that the division of stock
was unfair, and they heard the brothers ask for forgiveness.
The sisters then shared their resentments toward the brothers
who (although they were beneficiaries) were not responsible
for the initial injustice (after all, this was their father's decision).
Listening and requests for forgiveness were signs of true commitment to the process.

The family understood that meetings were a first step toward
reconciliation: nothing would be required other than listening
to each other. However, in everyone's mind was the question,
"Would something else be needed to heal frosty family relations?"
Although several outcomes were possible, the brothers renewed

their efforts to treat their sisters and their families as equals in all matters related to the ownership of the business. They agreed to ensure that voting shares were never used in making decisions. Instead, they agreed to use a consensus or a vote based on majority rule. For their part, the sisters did forgive their brothers (and ultimately their deceased father), and this freed them from resentment and an unproductive commitment to hold their brothers accountable for the past. Since then, their family relationships have become much healthier, and business decisions have become more productive.

Exhibit 4.4 lists a few basic steps necessary to begin moving toward reconciliation. It should be noted that each of these steps represents a high level of engagement and commitment by family members over time. While reconciliation is not intended to be a quick or easy fix, each family needs to approach it in a manner that makes sense for that particular family.

Where reconciliation is called for, it is often helpful to include an objective third party in the process. Third parties can help structure a reconciliation process, keep emotions in check, and help the family stay focused on the task at hand.

EXHIBIT 4.4   Steps That Lead to Reconciliation

- Step 1: Agree to address the problem.
- Step 2: Share individual perspectives on "the truth."
- Step 3: Identify and own your assumptions that support your truth.

- Step 4: Practice giving and receiving forgiveness:
  - Forgive to release yourself; holding a grudge takes a great deal of energy.
  - Use forgiveness as a tool to disarm anger and resentment and keep these feelings in their proper place.
  - Understand that forgiveness means looking forward while leaving the past where it belongs.
  - Recognize that forgiving in no way means that the event that caused the wound was okay.
  - Keep in mind that forgiveness doesn't mean giving up your sense of right and wrong.
  - When practicing forgiveness, *learn* from past hurts rather than forgetting them.

The previous example illustrated a process for reconciliation that can apply to family conflicts that have resulted in a cutoff. Sometimes a cutoff might have to be managed by the next-generation family members, who were not involved in the original event and who may have better relationships with each other than their parents ever did.

The essential elements in managing cutoffs include

- recognizing that relationships deserve to be salvaged,
- remaining calm to reduce emotionality, and
- either committing to a process of really listening to each other if the hurts are still raw and present or committing to letting go—that is, letting bygones be bygones and forgiving each other in the interest of preserving the relationship.

One closing comment about past injustices and cutoffs is called for here: a discussion of conflicts that include abuse or physical endangerment is beyond the scope of this book. In that light, we do want to note that sometimes emotional cutoffs are appropriate if a continuing relationship may be dangerous physically or psychologically for one or both parties involved. If these circumstances are suspected, it is best to seek assistance from a qualified mental health care professional.

> Staying calm sets a good tone for everybody involved; emotions are "contagious," so someone who is angry is likely to elicit an angry response from others.

FINAL THOUGHTS: SOME DILEMMAS SIMPLY REMAIN DILEMMAS

Unfortunately, the reality is that some conflicts simply don't have solutions or cannot be solved in the same environment in which they developed. There has been so much water under the bridge, or so many cycles of victimization have been perpetrated, or so little energy or interest in problem-solving remains that conflict management or resolution are just no longer possible. These situations are often marked by feelings of contempt: disdaining, disrespecting, and despising another person. Once relationships between family members deteriorate to the point that people feel *contempt* toward each other, it's very rare that those feelings can be reversed within the context of the family business. (Family therapists report a similar dynamic about married couples: that it's very difficult, if not impossible, to repair a marriage where the spouses feel contempt for each other. It's extremely rare for those couples to reconcile because contempt is such a negative and hateful emotion.)

The best solution very likely is for one or both family members involved to find a way to make a graceful exit from the business and open the door for improved relationships in the future.

Other situations that are difficult to resolve without a significant change in circumstances include the following:

- *A family member working in the business is incompetent for the task at hand.* When a family member is responsible for an aspect of the family business for which he or she truly isn't qualified or skilled or is not even competent to handle, no amount of talking and communicating will make that person more competent. And in that situation the person needs to engage in an education or mentoring program, accept a demotion, or leave the business.

- *Substance abuse or other addictive behavior.* A family member whose thought processes and behavior have been compromised by drugs or alcohol abuse, sex addiction, gambling, etc. will continue to create difficulties that jeopardize himself or herself, the family firm, and the family itself unless medical and mental health interventions are engaged.

Additional References

Aronoff, Craig E., Joseph H. Astrachan, Drew S. Mendoza, and John L. Ward. 2011. *Making Sibling Teams Work: The Next Generation.* New York: Palgrave Macmillan/Family Business Consulting Group.

Aronoff, Craig E., Joseph H. Astrachan, and John L. Ward. 2011. *Developing Family Business Policies: Your Guide to the Future.* New York: Palgrave Macmillan/Family Business Consulting Group.

Aronoff, Craig E., Stephen L. McClure, and John L. Ward. 2011. *Family Business Succession: The Final Test of Greatness.* New York: Palgrave Macmillan/Family Business Consulting Group.

Aronoff, Craig E., Stephen L. McClure, and John L. Ward. 2010. *Family Business Compensation.* New York: Palgrave Macmillan/Family Business Consulting Group.

Aronoff, Craig E., and John L. Ward. 2011. *Family Business Governance: Maximizing Family and Business Potential.* New York: Palgrave Macmillan/Family Business Consulting Group.

Aronoff, Craig E., and John L. Ward. 2011. *Family Business Ownership: How to Be an Effective Shareholder.* New York: Palgrave Macmillan/Family Business Consulting Group.

Aronoff, Craig E., and John L. Ward. 2011. *Family Meetings: How to Build a Stronger Family and a Stronger Business.* New York: Palgrave Macmillan/Family Business Consulting Group.

Covey, Stephen R. 2004. *The 7 Habits of Highly Effective People.* New York: Free Press.

Davis, J. A., and R. Tagiuri. 1982. *Bivalent Attributes of the Family Firm.* Santa Barbara, CA.: Owner Managed Business Institute.

Jung, Carl. (1938) 1958. "Psychology and Religion." In *Psychology and Religion: West and East*. Vol. II of *Collected Works*. London: Routledge and Kegan Paul.

Pendergast, Jennifer M., John L. Ward, and Stephanie Brun de Pontet. 2011. *Building a Successful Family Business Board: A Guide for Leaders, Directors, and Families*. Palgrave Macmillan/Family Business Consulting Group.

About the Authors

Dr. Kent Rhodes is a member of the Family Business Consulting Group, where he works with some of the most effective family-owned enterprises in the world, helping them navigate continuity planning, sibling/cousin team success, strategic change, and conflict management. A successful entrepreneur, Kent founded and later negotiated the sale of a thriving e-learning company and has served on corporate and nonprofit boards. He is a recognized expert in the field of organizational development, serving as core faculty with Pepperdine University's Graziadio School of Business and Management in Malibu, California.

Dr. David Lansky is a principal consultant with the Family Business Consulting Group, where he has played a key role in the growth and transformation of many enterprising families. A clinical psychologist and family therapist by training, David spent over 15 years in a clinical psychology practice, where he observed the impact that personal relationships, family dynamics, and communication obstacles can have on families' abilities to work, plan, and live well together. With his deep understanding of family dynamics, his unique ability to address critical individual and family concerns, and his appreciation for the challenges that accompany family wealth and family business, David helps to facilitate growth in families, repair difficult relationships, and turn stagnant or struggling enterprises into thriving organizations.

Index

abuse, 98
active listening, 58–61, 77
"aha" moments, 19
aligning vision and mission to
    manage future tensions, 84
amping up, 91
Aronoff, Craig, 24
assumptions, 53–54, 56–60, 96

bad habits, avoiding transfer of,
    89–93
barreling through, 92
being nice, 91
blaming, 92
bullying, 35, 37–39

CEOs, 13, 15–16, 19, 24, 35,
    54, 62
collaboration, 12, 18, 41, 44, 72, 85
communication
    active listening and, 58–61
    avoiding, 11
    clarity of, 89
    competence and, 99
    conflict and, 31–32, 35–36, 74
    indirect, 92
    meetings and, 45, 82
    between parents and
      children, 56–57

among siblings, 43, 95
staying calm and, 70
steps to better
    communication, 75
stopping, 87–88
compensation and ownership
    avoiding conflict, 27–33
    bullying and scapegoating,
      37–39
    opportunity and privilege,
      46–49
    overview, 23–26
    reducing conflict over, 26
    sibling rivalry, 40–46
    triangulation, 33–37
compromise, 18–19, 49
conflict management
    aligning vision and mission
      to manage future
      tensions, 84
    assessing skills, 57–58
    assumptions and, 53–57
    business first vs. family first,
      68–70
    core goals for, 5
    eight steps to better
      communication, 75
    ensuring clear and fair
      processes, 61–63

conflict management—
   Continued
   establishing policies and
      structures that benefit
      family and business,
      67–68
   ground ruled for family
      meetings, 76–77
   key elements to ensuring a
      fair process, 64
   practicing active listening,
      58–61
   small shifts that make a
      difference, 70–76
   utilizing structure, 63–68
conflicts
   avoiding, 27–33
   eliminating vs. managing,
      18–20
   reasons for, 10
conflicts of interest, avoiding, 64
consensus, 64
core goals for managing
      conflicts, 5
   see also conflict management
Covey, Stephen, 59

destructive entitlement , 84–87
diversity, understanding and
      accepting, 72–73
divorce, 11, 18

emotional cutoffs
   explained, 87–88
   reconciling, 97–98
employment, 26, 63, 68
ensuring clear and fair
      processes, 61–63

entitlement, 47, 84–88, 93
expectations, managing, 45,
      65, 69

fair processes, key elements to
      ensuring, 64
family constitutions, 62, 68
family meetings, ground rules
      for, 76–77
   see also meetings

governance, 45, 63, 65, 72

in-laws, 20, 72
inclusiveness, 72
incompetence, 99
indirect communication, 92
intellectualizing, 92
intimacy paradox, 11

Jung, Carl, 29

legacy, creating
   aligning vision and mission
      to manage future
      tensions, 84
   avoiding bad habits,
      89–93
   being aware of how history
      repeats itself, 87–89
   conflicts that cannot be
      resolved, 98–99
   overview, 81–84
   steps to aid in managing
      conflicts more
      effectively, 89
listening
   see active listening

marriage, 18, 99
McClure, Stephen, 24
meetings
    avoiding conflict and, 31–33
    conflict management and,
        28, 89
    ground rules for, 76–77
    inclusiveness and, 72
    managing effectively, 73–76
    policies and, 68
    privacy and, 31
    sibling rivalry and, 45, 95
    time management and, 31
    see also scheduling meetings

opportunity and privilege,
    46–49

philanthropy, 4, 9, 44, 48,
    63, 82
policies
    compensation and, 25, 65
    conflict management and, 17,
        45, 62, 89
    decision-making and, 69–70
    setting up, 65–68
    structure and, 63
privacy, 31, 75, 77

reconciliation, 93–98
    steps leading to, 96–97

saving face, 92
scapegoating, 37–39
scheduling meetings, 30–31
    see also meetings
sibling rivalry
    avoiding, 43–44
    beginnings of, 40–41
    business and, 41–42
    how to minimize, 45–46
    nature/nurture and, 42–43
    overview, 40
staying calm, 70–71
structure, utilizing, 63–68
substance abuse, 99

third-party facilitators, 30,
    33–34, 37, 96
three domains of family
        business, 15–18
    boundaries and, 16–17
    figure illustrating, 16
    managing, 17
triangulation, 33–37
    explained, 33–34
    five unwanted effects of, 34
    guidelines for managing,
        36–37

Ward, John L., 24
working with family,
    challenges of, 10

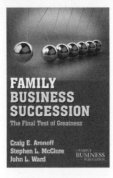

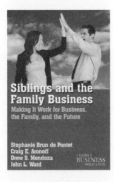